Presented To:

The Gilson family

Given By:

The Guenin family

On the Date Of:

Christmas 2014

*Be conscientious about yourself
and your teaching; persevere in these things,
for by doing this you will save both
yourself and your hearers.*

—

1 Timothy 4:16 HCSB

PROMISES
and
Prayers

$$1 + 1 = 2$$

for a dedicated teacher

The quoted ideas expressed in this book (but not Scripture verses) are not, in all cases, exact quotations, as some have been edited for clarity and brevity. In all cases, the author has attempted to maintain the speaker's original intent. In some cases, quoted material for this book was obtained from secondary sources, primarily print media. While every effort was made to ensure the accuracy of these sources, the accuracy cannot be guaranteed. For additions, deletions, corrections, or clarifications in future editions of this text, please write Freeman-Smith.

The Holy Bible, King James Version

The Holy Bible, New King James Version (NKJV) Copyright © 1982 by Thomas Nelson, Inc. Used by permission.

New century Version®. (NCV) Copyright © 1987, 1988, 1991 by Word Publishing, a division of Thomas Nelson, Inc. All rights reserved. Used by permission.

The Holman Christian Standard Bible™ (HCSB) Copyright © 1999, 2000, 2001 by Holman Bible Publishers. Used by permission.

The Holy Bible, New International Version®. (NIV) Copyright © 1973, 1978, 1984 International Bible Society. Used by permission of Zondervan. All rights reserved.

The Holy Bible. New Living Translation (NLT) copyright © 1996 Tyndale Charitable Trust. Used by permission of Tyndale House Publishers.

The New American Standard Bible®, (NASB) Copyright © 1960, 1962, 1963, 1968, 1971, 1972, 1973, 1975, 1977, 1995 by The Lockman Foundation. Used by permission.

Scripture taken from The Message. (MSG) Copyright © 1993, 1994, 1995, 1996, 2000, 2001, 2002. Used by permission of NavPress Publishing Group.

Cover Design by Kim Russell / Wahoo Designs
Page Layout by Bart Dawson

ISBN 978-1-60587-432-6

Printed in the United States of America

1 2 3 4 5—CHG—16 15 14 13 12

PROMISES
and
Prayers

$$1 + 1 = 2$$

for a dedicated teacher

TABLE OF CONTENTS

INTRODUCTION

Henry Adams correctly observed, "A teacher affects eternity; he can never tell where his influence stops." And, those words have never been more true than they are today. We live in a difficult, fast-paced, temptation-filled world; more than ever, our young people need the direction and the leadership provided by teachers who walk with God.

This text provides helpful reminders for the everyday challenges that face today's teachers. Whether you teach graduate school or Sunday School, whether you lecture at seminary or at Vacation Bible School, you are on an important journey with God . . . so you need and deserve a regularly scheduled conference with the ultimate Teacher. After all, you are God's emissary, a person charged with molding lives—a truly awesome responsibility. God takes your teaching duties very seriously, and so should you.

So, if you are fortunate enough to find yourself in the role of teacher, accept a hearty congratulations and a profound word of thanks. And then, for the next 30 days, take a few minutes each morning to consider the devotional readings on these pages. Remember that God honors your profession just as surely as He offers His loving abundance to you and your students. With God's help, you are destined to reshape eternity. It's a big job, but don't worry; you and God, working together, can handle it.

DAY 1

USING YOUR TALENTS

*I remind you to keep ablaze the gift of God
that is in you.*

—

2 Timothy 1:6 HCSB

As a teacher, your profession places you in a position of profound responsibility: you help mold the minds and lives of your students. Daniel Webster wrote: "If we work in marble, it will perish; if we work upon brass, time will efface it; if we rear temples, they will crumble into dust; but if we work upon immortal minds and instill in them just principles, we are then engraving upon tablets which no time will efface, but which will brighten and brighten to all eternity."

These words point out the opportunities that are available to talented teachers like you. And make no mistake—God knew precisely what He was doing when He gave you a unique set of talents and opportunities. And now, God wants you to use those talents for the glory of His kingdom. So here's the question: will you choose to use those talents?

Being a godly teacher in today's difficult world requires insight, discipline, patience, and prayer. May you, with God's help, use your talents to touch the hearts and minds of your students and, in doing so, refashion this wonderful world . . . and the next.

Wisdom from God's Holy Word

According to the grace given to us, we have different gifts: If prophecy, use it according to the standard of faith; if service, in service; if teaching, in teaching; if exhorting, in exhortation; giving, with generosity; leading, with diligence; showing mercy, with cheerfulness.

Romans 12:6-8 HCSB

His master said to him, "Well done, good and faithful slave! You were faithful over a few things; I will put you in charge of many things. Enter your master's joy!"

Matthew 25:21 HCSB

Every good gift and every perfect gift is from above, and cometh down from the Father of lights.

James 1:17 KJV

Now there are different gifts, but the same Spirit. There are different ministries, but the same Lord.

1 Corinthians 12:4-5 HCSB

More Great Ideas

You are a unique blend of talents, skills, and gifts, which makes you an indispensable member of the body of Christ.

Charles Stanley

Natural abilities are like natural plants; they need pruning by study.

Francis Bacon

You are the only person on earth who can use your ability.

Zig Ziglar

In the great orchestra we call life, you have an instrument and a song, and you owe it to God to play them both sublimely.

Max Lucado

Not everyone possesses boundless energy or a conspicuous talent. We are not equally blessed with great intellect or physical beauty or emotional strength. But we have all been given the same ability to be faithful.

Gigi Graham Tchividjian

If you want to reach
your potential,
you need to add a strong
work ethic to your talent.

—

John Maxwell

Today's Timely Tip

Converting raw talent into polished skill usually requires work, and lots of it. God's Word clearly instructs you to do the hard work of refining your talents for the glory of His kingdom and the service of His people. So, we are wise to remember the old adage: "What you are is God's gift to you; what you become is your gift to God." And it's up to you to make sure that your gift is worthy of the Giver.

Today's Prayer

Lord, You have given all of us talents, and I am no exception. You have blessed me with a gift—let me discover it, nurture it, and use it to the glory of Your Kingdom. Today, let me be a good and faithful steward, Father, of my talents and my possessions. Let me share my gifts with the world, and let me offer praise to You, the Giver of all things good. Amen

TRUST GOD'S PROMISES

*Man shall not live by bread alone,
but by every word that proceeds
from the mouth of God.*

—

Matthew 4:4 NKJV

I s God's Word a lamp that guides your be-havior in the classroom and beyond? Is God's Word your indispensable compass for everyday living, or is it relegated to Sunday morning services? Do you read the Bible faith-fully or sporadically? The answers to these questions will determine the direction of your thoughts, the direction of your day, and the direction of your life.

God's Word is unlike any other book. The Bible is a roadmap for life here on earth and for life eternal. As Christians, we are called upon to study God's Holy Word, to trust its promises, to follow its commandments, and to share its Good News with the world.

As believers, we must study the Bible and meditate upon its meaning for our lives. Oth-erwise, we deprive ourselves of a priceless gift from our Creator. God's Holy Word is, indeed, a transforming, life-changing, one-of-a-kind treasure. And, a passing acquaintance with the Good Book is insufficient for Christians who seek to obey God's Word and to under-stand His will. After all, neither man nor woman should live by bread alone . . .

Wisdom from God's Holy Word

But the word of the Lord endures forever. And this is the word that was preached as the gospel to you.

1 Peter 1:25 HCSB

All Scripture is inspired by God and is profitable for teaching, for rebuking, for correcting, for training in righteousness, so that the man of God may be complete, equipped for every good work.

2 Timothy 3:16-17 HCSB

For the word of God is living and effective and sharper than any two-edged sword, penetrating as far as to divide soul, spirit, joints, and marrow; it is a judge of the ideas and thoughts of the heart.

Hebrews 4:12 HCSB

The one who is from God listens to God's words. This is why you don't listen, because you are not from God.

John 8:47 HCSB

More Great Ideas

Either God's Word keeps you from sin, or sin keeps you from God's Word.

Corrie ten Boom

Weave the unveiling fabric of God's word through your heart and mind. It will hold strong, even if the rest of life unravels.

Gigi Graham Tchividjian

My meditation and study have shown me that, like God, His Word is holy, everlasting, absolutely true, powerful, personally fair, and never changing.

Bill Bright

Words fail to express my love for this holy Book, my gratitude for its author, for His love and goodness. How shall I thank him for it?

Lottie Moon

It takes calm, thoughtful, prayerful meditation on the Word to extract its deepest nourishment.

Vance Havner

I believe the reason so many
are failing today is that
they have not disciplined
themselves to read God's Word
consistently, day in and
day out, and to apply it to
every situation in life.

—

Kay Arthur

Today's Timely Tip

Never stop studying God's Word. Even if you've been studying the Bible for many years, you've still got lots to learn. Bible study should be a lifelong endeavor; make it your lifelong endeavor.

Today's Prayer

Heavenly Father, Your Holy Word is a light unto the world; let me share that Word with all who cross my path. Let me follow Your Son Jesus and be a fisher of men. Father, we live in a world that desperately needs Your saving grace. In all that I do, help me be a worthy witness for You as I share the Good News of Your perfect Son and Your perfect Word. Amen

YOUR MISSION

You reveal the path of life to me;
in Your presence is abundant joy;
in Your right hand are eternal pleasures.

—

Psalm 16:11 HCSB

Whether you realize it or not, you are on a personal mission for God. As a Christian teacher, that mission is straightforward: Honor your Creator, accept Christ as your Savior, teach your students truth, and serve those who cross your path.

Of course, you will encounter impediments as you attempt to discover the exact nature of God's purpose for your life, but you must never lose sight of the overriding purposes that God has established for all believers through the revelations of His Holy Word. When you apply God's commandments to every aspect of your life, you will earn countless blessings for yourself, your family, and your students.

Every day offers fresh opportunities to serve God, to worship Him, and to seek His will. When you do, He will bless you in miraculous ways. May you continue to seek God's purposes, may you trust His Word, and may you place Him where He belongs: at the very center of your life.

Wisdom from God's Holy Word

For it is God who is working among you both the willing and the working for His good purpose.

Philippians 2:13 HCSB

We know that all things work together for the good of those who love God: those who are called according to His purpose.

Romans 8:28 HCSB

Whatever you do, do everything for God's glory.

1 Corinthians 10:31 HCSB

Commit your activities to the Lord and your plans will be achieved.

Proverbs 16:3 HCSB

I will instruct you and show you the way to go; with My eye on you, I will give counsel.

Psalm 32:8 HCSB

More Great Ideas

The Christian life is not simply following principles but being empowered to fulfill our purpose: knowing and exalting Christ.

Franklin Graham

There is something about having endured great loss that brings purity of purpose and strength of character.

Barbara Johnson

We must always invite Jesus to be the navigator of our plans, desires, wills, and emotions, for He is the way, the truth, and the life.

Bill Bright

It's incredible to realize that what we do each day has meaning in the big picture of God's plan.

Bill Hybels

In the very place where God has put us, whatever its limitations, whatever kind of work it may be, we may indeed serve the Lord Christ.

Elisabeth Elliot

If the Lord calls you,
He will equip you for the task
He wants you to fulfill.

—

Warren Wiersbe

Today's Timely Tip

Ten years from now you will be somewhere—the question is where? You have the power to make that determination. And remember: it's not about earning a living; it's about designing a life.

Today's Prayer

Dear Lord, You are the Creator of the universe, and I know that Your plan for my life is grander than I can imagine. Let Your purposes be my purposes, and let me trust in the assurance of Your promises. Amen

SETTING THE RIGHT KIND OF EXAMPLE

*Set an example of good works yourself,
with integrity and dignity in your teaching.*

—

Titus 2:7 HCSB

Teachers serve as powerful examples to their students. Wise teachers understand that while words often fall upon closed ears, actions do not. And, godly teachers behave accordingly.

Life is a series of decisions and choices. Each day, we make countless decisions that can bring us closer to God . . . or not. When we live according to God's commandments, we earn for ourselves the abundance and peace that He intends for our lives. But, when we turn our backs upon God by disobeying Him, we bring needless suffering upon ourselves and our families.

Do you seek God's peace and His blessings? Then obey Him. When you're faced with a difficult choice or a powerful temptation, seek God's counsel and trust the counsel He gives. Invite God into your heart and live according to His commandments. When you do, you will be blessed—and your example will serve as a powerful blessing to your students, to your family, and to the world.

Wisdom from God's Holy Word

You should be an example to the believers in speech, in conduct, in love, in faith, in purity.

1 Timothy 4:12 HCSB

Do everything without grumbling and arguing, so that you may be blameless and pure.

Philippians 2:14–15 HCSB

For the kingdom of God is not in talk but in power.

1 Corinthians 4:20 HCSB

Therefore since we also have such a large cloud of witnesses surrounding us, let us lay aside every weight and the sin that so easily ensnares us, and run with endurance the race that lies before us.

Hebrews 12:1 HCSB

Do you see a man skilled in his work? He will stand in the presence of kings.

Proverbs 22:29 HCSB

More Great Ideas

You can never separate a leader's actions from his character.

John Maxwell

We urgently need people who encourage and inspire us to move toward God and away from the world's enticing pleasures.

Jim Cymbala

In our faith we follow in someone's steps. In our faith we leave footprints to guide others. It's the principle of discipleship.

Max Lucado

Living life with a consistent spiritual walk deeply influences those we love most.

Vonette Bright

Your light is the truth of the Gospel message itself as well as your witness as to Who Jesus is and what He has done for you. Don't hide it.

Anne Graham Lotz

Never support an experience
which does not have
God as its source and
faith in God as its result.

—

Oswald Chambers

Today's Timely Tip

Remember that actions speak more loudly than words. So it's not enough to talk about being a Christian; you must also demonstrate to students, friends, and family members precisely what it means to be a disciple of Christ.

Today's Prayer

Lord, let me be a righteous example to my students. Let me be honest and good, patient and kind, faithful to You and loving to others both now and forever. Amen

LEADERSHIP IN THE CLASSROOM

For an overseer, as God's manager, must be blameless, not arrogant, not quick tempered, not addicted to wine, not a bully, not greedy for money.

—

Titus 1:7 HCSB

As a teacher, you are automatically placed in a position of leadership. Unless, you assume firm control over your students, effective learning will not take place in your classroom.

John Maxwell writes, "Great leaders understand that the right attitude will set the right atmosphere, which enables the right response from others." As the leader of your class, it's up to you to set the proper balance between discipline and amusement, between entertainment and scholarship.

Savvy teachers learn to strike an appropriate balance between discipline (which is necessary for maintaining order) and fun (which is necessary for maintaining interest). The rest, of course, is up to the students.

Are you the kind of teacher whose class you would want to attend if you were a student? Hopefully so, because our world always needs another competent, Christ-centered leader . . . and so, for that matter, do your students.

Wisdom from God's Holy Word

According to the grace given to us, we have different gifts: If prophecy, use it according to the standard of faith; if service, in service; if teaching, in teaching; if exhorting, in exhortation; giving, with generosity; leading, with diligence; showing mercy, with cheerfulness.

Romans 12:6-8 HCSB

Shepherd God's flock among you, not overseeing out of compulsion but freely, according to God's will; not for the money but eagerly.

1 Peter 5:2 HCSB

And we exhort you, brothers: warn those who are lazy, comfort the discouraged, help the weak, be patient with everyone.

1 Thessalonians 5:14 HCSB

Those who are wise shall shine like the brightness of the firmament, and those who turn many to righteousness like the stars forever and ever.

Daniel 12:3 NKJV

More Great Ideas

A wise leader chooses a variety of gifted individuals. He complements his strengths.

Charles Stanley

True leaders are not afraid to surround themselves with people of ability—and not afraid to give those people opportunities for greatness.

Warren Wiersbe

Great leaders understand that the right attitude will set the right atmosphere, which enables the right response from others.

John Maxwell

A man ought to live so that everybody knows he is a Christian, and most of all, his family ought to know.

D. L. Moody

You can never separate a leader's actions from his character.

John Maxwell

Although our actions have
nothing to do with gaining
our own salvation,
they might be used by God
to save somebody else!
What we do really matters,
and it can affect the eternities
of people we care about.

—

Bill Hybels

Today's Timely Tip

Leadership comes in many forms, and you can lead others in your own way using your own style.

Today's Prayer

Dear Lord, when I find myself in a position of leadership, let me seek Your will and obey Your commandments. Make me a person of integrity and wisdom, Lord, and make me a worthy example to my students. Let me be a Christ-centered leader, and let me turn to You, Father, for guidance, for courage, for wisdom, and for love. Amen

CELEBRATING LIFE

This is the day the LORD has made;
we will rejoice and be glad in it.

—

Psalm 118:24 NKJV

Are you living a life of agitation, consternation, or celebration? If you're a believer, it should most certainly be the latter. With Christ as your Savior, every day should be a time of celebration.

Oswald Chambers correctly observed, "Joy is the great note all throughout the Bible." C. S. Lewis echoed that thought when he wrote, "Joy is the serious business of heaven." But, even the most dedicated Christians can, on occasion, forget to celebrate each day for what it is: a priceless gift from God.

Today, celebrate the life that God has given you. Today, put a smile on your face, kind words on your lips, and a song in your heart. Be generous with your praise and free with your encouragement. And then, when you have celebrated life to the fullest, invite your friends to do likewise. After all, this is God's day, and He has given us clear instructions for its use. We are commanded to rejoice and be glad. So, with no further ado, let the celebration begin . . .

Wisdom from God's Holy Word

Rejoice in the Lord always. I will say it again: Rejoice!

Philippians 4:4 HCSB

Their sorrow was turned into rejoicing and their mourning into a holiday. They were to be days of feasting, rejoicing, and of sending gifts to one another and the poor.

Esther 9:22 HCSB

At the dedication of the wall of Jerusalem, they sent for the Levites wherever they lived and brought them to Jerusalem to celebrate the joyous dedication with thanksgiving and singing accompanied by cymbals, harps, and lyres.

Nehemiah 12:27 HCSB

Rejoice and be exceedingly glad, for great is your reward in heaven.

Matthew 5:12 NKJV

More Great Ideas

Joy is the direct result of having God's perspective on our daily lives and the effect of loving our Lord enough to obey His commands and trust His promises.

Bill Bright

If you can forgive the person you were, accept the person you are, and believe in the person you will become, you are headed for joy. So celebrate your life.

Barbara Johnson

Some of us seem so anxious about avoiding hell that we forget to celebrate our journey toward heaven.

Philip Yancey

He wants us to have a faith that does not complain while waiting, but rejoices because we know our times are in His hands—nail-scarred hands that labor for our highest good.

Kay Arthur

The Christian lifestyle is not
one of legalistic
do's and don'ts, but one
that is positive, attractive,
and joyful.

—

Vonette Bright

Today's Timely Tip

Today is a cause for celebration: Psalm 118:24 has clear instructions for the coming day: "This is the day which the LORD has made; let us rejoice and be glad in it." Plan your day—and your life—accordingly.

Today's Prayer

Dear Lord, You have given me so many reasons to celebrate. Today, let me choose an attitude of cheerfulness. Let me be a joyful Christian, Lord, quick to laugh and slow to anger. And, let me share Your goodness with my family, my friends, my neighbors, and my students, this day and every day. Amen

THE POWER OF PERSEVERANCE

*For you need endurance, so that after
you have done God's will,
you may receive what was promised.*

—

Hebrews 10:36 HCSB

The familiar saying is true: "Life is a marathon, not a sprint." And, the same can be said of the teaching profession. Teaching requires determination, especially on those difficult days when the students are in an uproar and the lesson plan is in disarray.

In a world filled with roadblocks and stumbling blocks, we need strength, courage, and perseverance. And, as an example of perfect perseverance, we need look no further than our Savior, Jesus Christ. Our Savior finished what He began, and so must we.

Perhaps you are in a hurry for God to reveal His unfolding plans for your life. If so, be forewarned: God operates on His own timetable, not yours. Sometimes, God may answer your prayers with silence, and when He does, you must patiently persevere. In times of trouble, you must remain steadfast and trust in the merciful goodness of your Heavenly Father. Whatever your challenge, God can handle it. Your job is to keep persevering until He does.

Wisdom from God's Holy Word

Don't worry about anything, but in everything, through prayer and petition with thanksgiving, let your requests be made known to God.

Philippians 4:6 HCSB

Do you not know that the runners in a stadium all race, but only one receives the prize? Run in such a way that you may win. Now everyone who competes exercises self-control in everything. However, they do it to receive a perishable crown, but we an imperishable one.

1 Corinthians 9:24-25 HCSB

Pursue righteousness, godliness, faith, love, endurance, and gentleness. Fight the good fight for the faith; take hold of eternal life, to which you were called and have made a good confession before many witnesses.

1 Timothy 6:11-12 HCSB

But as for you, be strong; don't be discouraged, for your work has a reward.

2 Chronicles 15:7 HCSB

More Great Ideas

The hardest part of a journey is neither the start nor the finish, but the middle mile.

Vance Havner

Don't quit. For if you do, you may miss the answer to your prayers.

Max Lucado

Untold damage has been done to the cause of Christ because some people gear up for a sprint when they need to train for the marathon.

Bill Hybels

Let us not cease to do the utmost, that we may incessantly go forward in the way of the Lord; and let us not despair of the smallness of our accomplishments.

John Calvin

Jesus taught that perseverance is the essential element in prayer.

E. M. Bounds

We are all
on our way somewhere.
We'll get there
if we just keep going.

—

Barbara Johnson

Today's Timely Tip

Teaching, like life, is an exercise in perseverance. If you persevere, you will win . . . and so will your students.

Today's Prayer

Dear Lord, life is not a sprint, but a marathon. When the pace of my life becomes frantic, slow me down and give me perspective. Keep me steady and sure. When I become weary, let me persevere so that, in Your time, I might finish my work here on earth, and that You might then say, "Well done my good and faithful servant." Amen

WISE WORDS

Summoning the crowd, He told them,
"Listen and understand: It's not what goes into
the mouth that defiles a man, but what comes
out of the mouth, this defiles a man."

—

Matthew 15:10-11 HCSB

Think . . . pause . . . then speak: How wise is the teacher who can communicate in this way. But occasionally, amid the pressures of the school day, even the most considerate teacher may speak first and think next . . . with unfortunate results.

God's Word reminds us that "Reckless words pierce like a sword, but the tongue of the wise brings healing" (Proverbs 12:18 NIV). If we seek to be a source of encouragement to our students, to our peers, and to our families, then we must measure our words carefully. Words are important: they can hurt or heal. Words can uplift us or discourage us, and reckless words, spoken in haste, cannot be erased.

Today, seek to encourage all who cross your path. Measure your words carefully. Speak wisely, not impulsively. Use words of kindness and praise, not words of anger or derision. Remember that you have the power to heal others or to injure them, to lift others up or to hold them back. When you lift them up, your wisdom will bring healing and comfort to a classroom and a world that needs both.

Wisdom from God's Holy Word

Pleasant words are a honeycomb: sweet to the taste and health to the body.

Proverbs 16:24 HCSB

For the one who wants to love life and to see good days must keep his tongue from evil and his lips from speaking deceit.

1 Peter 3:10 HCSB

Avoid irreverent, empty speech, for this will produce an even greater measure of godlessness.

2 Timothy 2:16 HCSB

No rotten talk should come from your mouth, but only what is good for the building up of someone in need, in order to give grace to those who hear.

Ephesians 4:29 HCSB

The wise store up knowledge, but the mouth of the fool hastens destruction.

Proverbs 10:14 HCSB

More Great Ideas

I still believe we ought to talk about Jesus. The old country doctor of my boyhood days always began his examination by saying, "Let me see your tongue." That's a good way to check a Christian: the tongue test. Let's hear what he is talking about.

Vance Havner

Attitude and the spirit in which we communicate are as important as the words we say.

Charles Stanley

Change the heart, and you change the speech.

Warren Wiersbe

Part of good communication is listening with the eyes as well as with the ears.

Josh McDowell

It is time that the followers of Jesus revise their language and learn to speak respectfully of non-Christian peoples.

Lottie Moon

In all your deeds and words,
you should look on Jesus
as your model, whether you are
keeping silence or speaking,
whether you are alone
or with others.

—

St. Bonaventure

Today's Timely Tip

Trust God's Timing: God has very big plans in store for your life, so trust Him and wait patiently for those plans to unfold. And remember: God's timing is best, so don't allow yourself to become discouraged if things don't work out exactly as you wish. Instead of worrying about your future, entrust it to God. He knows exactly what you need and exactly when you need it.

Today's Prayer

Lord, You have commanded me to choose my words carefully so that I might be a source of encouragement and hope to all whom I meet. Keep me mindful, Father, that I have influence on many people, especially my students . . . make me an influence for good. And may the words that I speak today be worthy of the One who has saved me forever. Amen

THE POWER OF PATIENCE

Wait on the Lord, and He will rescue you.

—

Proverbs 20:22 HCSB

Students, even the most dedicated and well-intentioned, are far from perfect. They make mistakes and misbehave; they don't always listen, and they don't always complete their assignments. In an imperfect school filled with imperfect people, a teacher's patience is tested many times each day. But, God's instructions are clear: "be patient, bearing with one another in love" (Ephesians 4:2 NIV). As believers, we must exercise patience, even when doing so is difficult.

Teaching, like every job, has its fair share of frustrations—some great, and some small. Sometimes, these frustrations may cause you to reach the boiling point. But here's a word of warning: When you're tempted to lose your temper over the minor inconveniences of the teaching profession, don't give voice to your angry thoughts.

When you make haste to speak angry words, you will inevitably say things that you'll soon regret. Remember that God will help you control your temper if you ask Him to do so. And the time to ask for His help is *before* your temper gets the best of you.

Wisdom from God's Holy Word

Love is patient; love is kind.

1 Corinthians 13:4 HCSB

A patient spirit is better than a proud spirit.

Ecclesiastes 7:8 HCSB

Therefore, God's chosen ones, holy and loved, put on heartfelt compassion, kindness, humility, gentleness, and patience.

Colossians 3:12 HCSB

A patient person [shows] great understanding, but a quick-tempered one promotes foolishness.

Proverbs 14:29 HCSB

My dearly loved brothers, understand this: everyone must be quick to hear, slow to speak, and slow to anger, for man's anger does not accomplish God's righteousness.

James 1:19-20 HCSB

More Great Ideas

If God is diligent, surely we ought to be diligent in doing our duty to Him. Think how patient and diligent God has been to us!

Oswald Chambers

If you want to hear God's voice clearly and you are uncertain, then remain in His presence until He changes that uncertainty. Often much can happen during this waiting for the Lord. Sometimes he changes pride into humility; doubt into faith and peace . . . .

Corrie ten Boom

The challenge before us is to have faith in God, and the hardest part of faith is waiting.

Jim Cymbala

He makes us wait. He keeps us in the dark on purpose. He makes us walk when we want to run, sit still when we want to walk, for he has things to do in our souls that we are not interested in.

Elisabeth Elliot

God is in no hurry.
Compared to the works
of mankind, His is
extremely deliberate.
God is not a slave
to the human clock.

—

Charles Swindoll

Today's Timely Tip

If you think you're about to say or do something you'll regret later, slow down and take a deep breath, or two deep breaths, or ten, or . . . well you get the idea.

Today's Prayer

Make me a patient teacher, Lord, slow to anger and quick to forgive. When I am hurried, slow me down. When I become impatient with others, give me empathy. Today, let me be a patient servant as I trust in You, Father, and in Your master plan. Amen

DEPEND UPON HIS STRENGTH

I raise my eyes toward the mountains.
Where will my help come from?
My help comes from the Lord,
the Maker of heaven and earth.

—

Psalm 121:1-2 HCSB

As a dedicated teacher, you may experience moments when you feel overworked, overstressed, and underappreciated. Thankfully, God stands ready to renew your optimism and your strength if you turn to Him.

Because you are a teacher, you are helping to shape the lives of your students. Your work is profoundly important. Consider it God's work.

When you feel worried or weary, focus your thoughts upon God and upon His plans for you. Then, ask Him for the wisdom to prioritize your life. Finally, ask God for the strength and courage to fulfill your responsibilities.

When you sincerely seek to follow God's path for your life, you will become energized. And then, with God as your partner, you'll be amazed at the things that the two of you can accomplish.

Wisdom from God's Holy Word

Now the God of all grace, who called you to His eternal glory in Christ Jesus, will personally restore, establish, strengthen, and support you.

1 Peter 5:10 HCSB

The LORD is my strength and song, and He has become my salvation; He is my God, and I will praise Him . . .

Exodus 15:2 NKJV

Peace, peace to you, and peace to your helpers! For your God helps you.

1 Chronicles 12:18 NKJV

He gives power to the weak, and to those who have no might He increases strength.

Isaiah 40:29 NKJV

Take My yoke upon you and learn from Me, because I am gentle and humble in heart, and you will find rest for your souls. For My yoke is easy and My burden is light.

Matthew 11:29-30 HCSB

More Great Ideas

Once we recognize our need for Jesus, then the building of our faith begins. It is a daily, moment-by-moment life of absolute dependence upon Him for everything.

Catherine Marshall

Faith is not merely you holding on to God—it is God holding on to you.

E. Stanley Jones

He stands fast as your rock, steadfast as your safeguard, sleepless as your watcher, valiant as your champion.

C. H. Spurgeon

Measure the size of the obstacles against the size of God.

Beth Moore

God will never lead you where His strength cannot keep you.

Barbara Johnson

God does not promise to keep
us out of the storms and floods,
but He does promise to sustain
us in the storm, and then
bring us out in due time for
His glory when the storm
has done its work.

—

Warren Wiersbe

Today's Timely Tip

God can handle it. Corrie ten Boom advised, "God's all-sufficiency is a major. Your inability is a minor. Major in majors, not in minors." Enough said.

Today's Prayer

Dear Lord, as I face the challenges of this day, You protect me. I thank You, Father, for Your love and for Your strength. I will lean upon You today and forever. Amen

TAKING TIME TO GIVE THANKS

I will give You thanks with all my heart.

—

Psalm 138:1 HCSB

For most of us, life is busy and complicated. And, as teachers, we have countless responsibilities that begin long before the school bell rings and end long after the last student has left the classroom. Amid the rush and crush of the daily grind, it is easy to lose sight of God and His blessings. But, when we forget to slow down and say "Thank You" to our Maker, we rob ourselves of His presence, His peace, and His joy.

Instead of ignoring God, we should praise Him many times each day. Then, with gratitude in our hearts, we can face the day's complications with the perspective and power that only He can provide.

Wisdom from God's Holy Word

Give thanks to the Lord, for He is good; His faithful love endures forever.

Psalm 118:29 HCSB

Those who cling to worthless idols forsake faithful love, but as for me, I will sacrifice to You with a voice of thanksgiving. I will fulfill what I have vowed. Salvation is from the Lord!

Jonah 2:8-9 HCSB

And whatever you do, in word or in deed, do everything in the name of the Lord Jesus, giving thanks to God the Father through Him.

Colossians 3:17 HCSB

Therefore as you have received Christ Jesus the Lord, walk in Him, rooted and built up in Him and established in the faith, just as you were taught, and overflowing with thankfulness.

Colossians 2:6-7 HCSB

More Great Ideas

The heathen misrepresent God by worshipping idols; we misrepresent God by our murmuring and our complaining.

C. H. Spurgeon

Why wait until the fourth Thursday in November? Why wait until the morning of December twenty-fifth? Thanksgiving to God should be an everyday affair. The time to be thankful is now!

Jim Gallery

Contentment comes when we develop an attitude of gratitude for the important things we do have in our lives that we tend to take for granted if we have our eyes staring longingly at our neighbor's stuff.

Dave Ramsey

Let's thank God for allowing us to experience troubles that drive us closer to Him.

Shirley Dobson

It is only with gratitude
that life becomes rich.

—

Dietrich Bonhoeffer

Today's Timely Tip

Since you're thankful to God, tell Him so. And keep telling Him so every day of your life.

Today's Prayer

Heavenly Father, Your gifts are greater than I can imagine. May I live each day with thanksgiving in my heart and praise on my lips. Thank You for the gift of Your Son and for the promise of eternal life. Let me share the joyous news of Jesus Christ, and let my life be a testimony to His love and His grace. Amen

THE CLASSROOM'S GOLDEN RULE

*Therefore, whatever you want others
to do for you, do also the same for them—
this is the Law and the Prophets.*

—

Matthew 7:12 HCSB

Would you like to improve your classroom and your world? If so, you can start by practicing the Golden Rule.

Jesus said, "Do to others what you want them to do to you" (Matthew 7:12 NCV). That means that you should treat everyone (including your students) in the very same way that you want to be treated.

Is the Golden Rule your rule both inside and outside the classroom? Hopefully so. After all, Jesus made Himself perfectly clear: He instructed you to treat other people in the same way that you want to be treated—no exceptions.

So if you want to know how to respond to others, ask the person you see every time you look into the mirror. It's the decent way to teach and the decent way to live.

Wisdom from God's Holy Word

Just as you want others to do for you, do the same for them.

Luke 6:31 HCSB

See that no one renders evil for evil to anyone, but always pursue what is good both for yourselves and for all.

1 Thessalonians 5:15 NKJV

If you really carry out the royal law prescribed in Scripture, You shall love your neighbor as yourself, you are doing well.

James 2:8 HCSB

And let us not grow weary while doing good, for in due season we shall reap if we do not lose heart.

Galatians 6:9 NKJV

For we are His workmanship, created in Christ Jesus for good works, which God prepared beforehand that we should walk in them.

Ephesians 2:10 NKJV

More Great Ideas

Before you can dry another's tears, you too must weep.

Barbara Johnson

Do all the good you can. By all the means you can. In all the ways you can. In all the places you can. At all the times you can. To all the people you can. As long as ever you can.

John Wesley

The Golden Rule starts at home, but it should never stop there.

Marie T. Freeman

Faith never asks whether good works are to be done, but has done them before there is time to ask the question, and it is always doing them.

Martin Luther

It is one of the most beautiful compensations of life that no one can sincerely try to help another without helping herself.

Barbara Johnson

A cheerful giver does not count the cost of what he gives. His heart is set on pleasing and cheering him to whom the gift is given.

—

Juliana of Norwich

Today's Timely Tip

Remember this: when you treat others with respect, you won't just feel better about them, you'll feel better about yourself, too.

Today's Prayer

Dear Lord, let me teach the Golden Rule, and let me live by it. Because I expect kindness, let me be kind. Because I wish to be loved, let me be loving. Because I need forgiveness, let me be merciful. In all things, Lord, let me live by the Golden Rule that is the commandment of Your Son Jesus. Amen

ENCOUNTERING DIFFICULT PEOPLE

Hatred stirs up strife, but love covers all sins.

—

Proverbs 10:12 NKJV

All of us can be grumpy, hardheaded, and difficult to deal with at times. And as teachers, we must, from time to time, encounter out-of-sorts parents or their out-of-sorts offspring. When you have occasion to deal with difficult people (and you will), the following tips should help:

1. Don't Try to Change the Other Person: Why? Because teenagers and adults change when they want to, not when you want them to. (Proverbs 10:14)

2. Do Insist Upon Logical Consequences to Irresponsible Behavior: When you protect other people from the consequences of their misbehavior, you're doing those folks a profound disservice.

3. Don't Allow Yourself to Become Caught Up in the Other Person's Emotional Outbursts: Remember: emotions are highly contagious, so if the other person is angry, you will soon become angry, too. Instead of adding your own emotional energy to the outburst, you should make the conscious effort to remain calm—and part of remaining calm may be leaving the scene. (Proverbs 22:24-25)

And finally, when you've finished dealing with that difficult person, do your best to forget about the confrontation. Everybody's human, and everybody needs forgiveness. And that includes, parents, students, and—on rare occasions—teachers, too.

Wisdom from God's Holy Word

A contrary man spreads conflict, and a gossip separates friends.

Proverbs 16:28 HCSB

A person with great anger bears the penalty; if you rescue him, you'll have to do it again.

Proverbs 19:19 HCSB

Don't worry because of evildoers, and don't envy the wicked.

Proverbs 24:19 HCSB

Don't answer a fool according to his foolishness, or you'll be like him yourself.

Proverbs 26:4 HCSB

More Great Ideas

We are all fallen creatures and all very hard to live with.

C. S. Lewis

When something robs you of your peace of mind, ask yourself if it is worth the energy you are expending on it. If not, then put it out of your mind in an act of discipline. Every time the thought of "it" returns, refuse it.

Kay Arthur

You can be sure you are abiding in Christ if you are able to have a Christlike love toward the people that irritate you the most.

Vonette Bright

Sour godliness is the devil's religion.

John Wesley

If some hypocrites do intrude among us, it should not astonish us.

C. H. Spurgeon

To be a Christian means
to forgive the inexcusable,
because God has forgiven
the inexcusable in you.

—

C. S. Lewis

Today's Timely Tip

If a student or parent is ranting, raving, or worse, you have the right to get up and leave. Remember: emotions are highly contagious, so if the other person is angry, you will soon become angry, too. Instead of adding your own emotional energy to the outburst, you should make the conscious effort to remain calm—and part of remaining calm may be leaving the scene of the argument.

Today's Prayer

Heavenly Father, make me a kind person even to those who don't treat me kindly. Let me forgive others, just as You have forgiven me. Amen

BIG DREAMS

*But if we hope for what we do not see,
we eagerly wait for it with patience.*

—

Romans 8:25 HCSB

Are you willing to entertain the possibility that God has big plans in store for you as well as your students? Hopefully so. Yet sometimes, especially if you've recently experienced a life-altering disappointment, you may find it difficult to envision the possibility of a brighter future. If so, it's time to stop placing limitations upon yourself, upon your students, and upon God.

Your Heavenly Father created you with unique gifts and untapped talents; your job is to tap them. When you do, you'll begin to feel an increasing sense of confidence in yourself and in your future. Then, you can share that confidence with your students, with your family, and with your friends.

It takes courage to dream big dreams. You will discover that courage when you do three things: accept the past, trust God to handle the future, and make the most of the time He has given you today.

Nothing is too difficult for God, and no dreams are too big for Him—not even yours. So start living—and dreaming—accordingly.

Wisdom from God's Holy Word

Happy is he who has the God of Jacob for his help, whose hope is in the Lord his God.

Psalm 146:5 NKJV

The Lord values those who fear Him, those who put their hope in His faithful love.

Psalm 147:11 HCSB

May He grant you according to your heart's desire, and fulfill all your purpose.

Psalm 20:4 NKJV

Lord, I turn my hope to You. My God, I trust in You. Do not let me be disgraced; do not let my enemies gloat over me.

Psalm 25:1-2 HCSB

Rejoice in hope; be patient in affliction; be persistent in prayer.

Romans 12:12 HCSB

More Great Ideas

Always stay connected to people and seek out things that bring you joy. Dream with abandon. Pray confidently.

Barbara Johnson

The future lies all before us. Shall it only be a slight advance upon what we usually do? Ought it not to be a bound, a leap forward to altitudes of endeavor and success undreamed of before?

Annie Armstrong

Set goals so big that unless God helps you, you will be a miserable failure.

Bill Bright

You cannot out-dream God.

John Eldredge

To make your dream come true, you have to stay awake.

Dennis Swanberg

Faith looks back and
draws courage;
hope looks ahead and
keeps desire alive.

—

John Eldredge

Today's Timely Tip

Making your dreams come true requires work. John Maxwell writes, "The gap between your vision and your present reality can only be filled through a commitment to maximize your potential." Enough said.

Today's Prayer

Dear Lord, give me the courage to dream and the wisdom to help my students do likewise. When I am worried or weary, give me strength for today and hope for tomorrow. Keep me mindful of Your miraculous power, Your infinite love, and Your eternal salvation. Amen

THE POWER OF ENTHUSIASM

*Whatever you do, do it enthusiastically,
as something done for the Lord and not for men.*

—

Colossians 3:23 HCSB

A re you enthusiastic about your life and your faith? Hopefully so. But if your zest for life has waned, it is now time to redirect your efforts and recharge your spiritual batteries. And that means refocusing your priorities (by putting God first) and counting your blessings (instead of your troubles).

Nothing is more important than your wholehearted commitment to your Creator and to His only begotten Son. Your faith must never be an afterthought; it must be your ultimate priority, your ultimate possession, and your ultimate passion. When you become passionate about your faith, you'll become passionate about your life, too.

If you're a teacher with too many obligations and too few hours in which to meet them, you are not alone. Teaching can be a demanding profession. But don't fret. Instead, focus upon God and upon His love for you. Then, ask Him for the strength you need to fulfill your responsibilities. God will give you the enthusiasm to do the most important things on today's to-do list . . . if you ask Him.

Wisdom from God's Holy Word

Until now you have asked for nothing in My name. Ask and you will receive, that your joy may be complete.

John 16:24 HCSB

Now I am coming to You, and I speak these things in the world so that they may have My joy completed in them.

John 17:13 HCSB

And suddenly there was with the angel a multitude of the heavenly host praising God and saying: "Glory to God in the highest, And on earth peace, goodwill toward men!"

Luke 2:13-14 NKJV

Glory in His holy name; let the hearts of those rejoice who seek the Lord! Seek the Lord and His strength; seek His face evermore!

1 Chronicles 16:10-11 NKJV

More Great Ideas

When we wholeheartedly commit ourselves to God, there is nothing mediocre or run-of-the-mill about us. To live for Christ is to be passionate about our Lord and about our lives.

Jim Gallery

Don't take hold of a thing unless you want that thing to take hold of you.

E. Stanley Jones

Enthusiasm, like the flu, is contagious—we get it from one another.

Barbara Johnson

Wherever you are, be all there. Live to the hilt every situation you believe to be the will of God.

Jim Elliot

One of the great needs in the church today is for every Christian to become enthusiastic about his faith in Jesus Christ.

Billy Graham

Think enthusiastically
about everything,
especially your work.

—

Norman Vincent Peale

Today's Timely Tip

Don't wait for enthusiasm to find you . . . go looking for it. Look at your life and your classroom as exciting adventures. Don't wait for life to spice itself; spice things up yourself.

Today's Prayer

Lord, when the classroom leaves me exhausted, let me turn to You for strength and for renewal. When I follow Your will for my life, You will renew my enthusiasm. Let Your will be my will, Lord, and let me find my strength in You. Amen

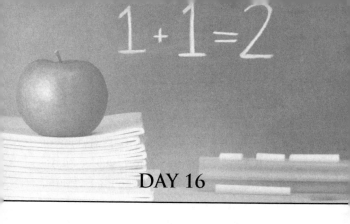

HOPE FOR TODAY

*Sustain me as You promised, and I will live;
do not let me be ashamed of my hope.*

—

Psalm 119:116 HCSB

Along with other lessons, we must teach our students the wisdom of hope. There are few sadder sights than that of a thoroughly discouraged young person. As teachers, we cannot control the emotions of our students, but we can help our students learn to think optimistically about themselves and about their opportunities.

Hope, like plants in a garden, must be cultivated with care. If we leave our hopes untended—or if we contaminate them with the twin poisons of discouragement and doubt—the gardens of our souls produce few fruits. But, if we nurture our hopes through a firm faith in God and a realistic faith in ourselves, we bring forth bountiful harvests that bless us, our families, ours students, and generations yet unborn.

Wisdom from God's Holy Word

Let us hold on to the confession of our hope without wavering, for He who promised is faithful.

Hebrews 10:23 HCSB

Now may the God of hope fill you with all joy and peace in believing, so that you may overflow with hope by the power of the Holy Spirit.

Romans 15:13 HCSB

Rejoice in hope; be patient in affliction; be persistent in prayer.

Romans 12:12 HCSB

Lord, I turn my hope to You. My God, I trust in You. Do not let me be disgraced; do not let my enemies gloat over me.

Psalm 25:1-2 HCSB

Delayed hope makes the heart sick.

Proverbs 13:12 HCSB

More Great Ideas

Earth's best is only a dim reflection and a preliminary rendering of the glory that will one day be revealed.

Joni Eareckson Tada

Easter comes each year to remind us of a truth that is eternal and universal. The empty tomb of Easter morning says to you and me, "Of course you'll encounter trouble. But behold a God of power who can take any evil and turn it into a door of hope."

Catherine Marshall

Teach us to set our hopes on heaven, to hold firmly to the promise of eternal life, so that we can withstand the struggles and storms of this world.

Max Lucado

Love is the seed of all hope. It is the enticement to trust, to risk, to try, and to go on.

Gloria Gaither

Everything that is done
in the world is done by hope.

—

Martin Luther

Today's Timely Tip

Never be afraid to hope—or to ask—for a miracle.

Today's Prayer

Dear Lord, make me a teacher of hope. If I become discouraged, let me turn to You. If I grow weary, let me seek strength in You. When I face adversity, let me seek Your will and trust Your Word. In every aspect of my life, I will trust You, Father, so that my heart will be filled with faith and hope, this day and forever. Amen

TEACHING DISCIPLINE

No discipline seems enjoyable at the time, but painful. Later on, however, it yields the fruit of peace and righteousness to those who have been trained by it.

—

Hebrews 12:11 HCSB

As a teacher, you are charged with a thankless task: controlling students who would prefer not to be controlled. Hopefully, your students will learn that disciplined behavior is a prerequisite for success both inside and outside the classroom.

Those who study the Bible are confronted again and again with God's intention that His children (of all ages) lead disciplined lives. God doesn't reward laziness or misbehavior. To the contrary, He expects His own to adopt a disciplined approach to their lives, and He punishes those who disobey His commandments.

Do you teach the importance of discipline? If so, many of your students are learning powerful, life-changing lessons about the rewards of a disciplined lifestyle. And rest assured that your example will speak far more loudly than your lectures. So teach the fine art of responsible behavior through your words and your actions, but not necessarily in that order.

Wisdom from God's Holy Word

But each person should examine his own work, and then he will have a reason for boasting in himself alone, and not in respect to someone else. For each person will have to carry his own load.

Galatians 6:4-5 HCSB

For this very reason, make every effort to supplement your faith with goodness, goodness with knowledge, knowledge with self-control, self-control with endurance, endurance with godliness.

2 Peter 1:5-6 HCSB

I discipline my body and bring it under strict control, so that after preaching to others, I myself will not be disqualified.

1 Corinthians 9:27 HCSB

And God is able to make every grace overflow to you, so that in every way, always having everything you need, you may excel in every good work.

2 Corinthians 9:8 HCSB

More Great Ideas

If I could just hang in there, being faithful to my own tasks, God would make me joyful and content. The responsibility is mine, but the power is His.

Peg Rankin

The Bible calls for discipline and a recognition of authority. Children must learn this at home.

Billy Graham

Discipline is training that develops and corrects.

Charles Stanley

Work is doing it. Discipline is doing it every day. Diligence is doing it well every day.

Dave Ramsey

The alternative to discipline is disaster.

Vance Havner

Discipline is the refining fire
by which talent
becomes ability.

—

Roy L. Smith

Today's Timely Tip

Expect your students to be well-behaved, but don't expect them to be perfect. In fact, an important part of teaching is knowing what to overlook and when to overlook it.

Today's Prayer

Dear Lord, Your Holy Word tells us that You expect Your children to be diligent and disciplined. You have told us that the fields are ripe and the workers are few. Lead me to Your fields, Lord, and make me a disciplined teacher in the service of Your Son, Christ Jesus. When I am weary, give me strength. When I am discouraged, give me hope. Make me a disciplined, courageous, industrious servant for Your Kingdom today and forever. Amen

THE POWER OF KINDNESS

*And may the Lord make you increase
and abound in love to one another and to all.*

—

1 Thessalonians 3:12 NKJV

In the busyness and stress of a teacher's demanding day, it is easy to become frustrated. We are imperfect human beings struggling to manage our lives as best we can, but sometimes we fall short. When we are distracted or disappointed, we may neglect to share a kind word or a kind deed. This oversight hurts others, and it hurts us as well.

Christ's commandment is clear: Matthew 25:40 warns, "Verily I say unto you, Inasmuch as ye have done it unto one of the least of these my brethren, ye have done it unto me" (KJV). When we share a word of encouragement with a student or extend the hand of friendship to a peer, God promises His blessings. When we ignore the needs of others—or mistreat them—we risk God's retribution.

Today, slow yourself down and be alert for those who need your smile, your kind words, or your helping hand. Make kindness a centerpiece of your dealings with others. They will be blessed, and so will you.

Wisdom from God's Holy Word

Finally, all of you be of one mind, having compassion for one another; love as brothers, be tenderhearted, be courteous.

1 Peter 3:8 NKJV

And be kind and compassionate to one another, forgiving one another, just as God also forgave you in Christ.

Ephesians 4:32 HCSB

Carry one another's burdens; in this way you will fulfill the law of Christ.

Galatians 6:2 HCSB

Pure and undefiled religion before our God and Father is this: to look after orphans and widows in their distress and to keep oneself unstained by the world.

James 1:27 HCSB

A kind man benefits himself, but a cruel man brings disaster on himself.

Proverbs 11:17 HCSB

More Great Ideas

When you extend hospitality to others, you're not trying to impress people, you're trying to reflect God to them.

Max Lucado

All kindness and good deeds, we must keep silent. The result will be an inner reservoir of personality power.

Catherine Marshall

If we have the true love of God in our hearts, we will show it in our lives. We will not have to go up and down the earth proclaiming it. We will show it in everything we say or do.

D. L. Moody

It is one of the most beautiful compensations of life that no one can sincerely try to help another without helping herself.

Barbara Johnson

Be so preoccupied with good will that you haven't room for ill will.

E. Stanley Jones

One of the greatest things
a man can do for his
Heavenly Father is to be kind
to some of his other children.

—

Henry Drummond

Today's Timely Tip

Kindness matters: When you make the decision to be a genuinely kind person, you'll make decisions that improve your own life and the lives of your students, your family, and your friends.

Today's Prayer

Lord, make me a loving, encouraging Christian. And, let my love for Christ be reflected through the kindness that I show to my students, to my family, to my friends, and to all who need the healing touch of the Master's hand. Amen

WHEN TIMES ARE TOUGH

Whatever has been born of God conquers the world. This is the victory that has conquered the world: our faith.

—

1 John 5:4 HCSB

Teachers of every generation have experienced challenges, and this generation is no different. But, today's teachers face difficulties that previous generations could have scarcely imagined. Thankfully, although the world continues to change, God's love remains constant. And, He remains ready to comfort us and strengthen us whenever we turn to Him.

Because we human beings have the ability to think, we also have the ability to worry. All of us, even the most faithful believers, are plagued by occasional periods of discouragement and doubt. Even though we hold tightly to God's promise of salvation—even though we believe sincerely in God's love and protection—we may find ourselves fretting over the countless details of everyday life. We worry about health, about finances, about safety, about relationships, about family, and about countless other challenges, some great and some small.

Where is the best place to take our worries? We should take them to God. We should take our troubles to Him, our fears, our dilemmas, and our sorrows. We should seek protection from the One who cannot be moved. Then, when we have genuinely turned our concerns over to God, we should worry less and trust Him more, because God is trustworthy . . . and we are protected.

Wisdom from God's Holy Word

When you are in distress and all these things have happened to you, you will return to the Lord your God in later days and obey Him. He will not leave you, destroy you, or forget the covenant with your fathers that He swore to them by oath, because the Lord your God is a compassionate God.

Deuteronomy 4:30-31 HCSB

Dear friends, when the fiery ordeal arises among you to test you, don't be surprised by it, as if something unusual were happening to you. Instead, as you share in the sufferings of the Messiah rejoice, so that you may also rejoice with great joy at the revelation of His glory.

1 Peter 4:12-13 HCSB

More Great Ideas

Christians are like tea bags. It's only when they get into hot water that you find out how strong they are.

Anonymous

Suffering will be either your master or your servant, depending on how you handle the crises of life.

Warren Wiersbe

Measure the size of the obstacles against the size of God.

Beth Moore

Through all of the crises of life—and we all are going to experience them—we have this magnificent Anchor.

Franklin Graham

The Lord gets his best soldiers out of the highlands of affliction.

C. H. Spurgeon

The only way to learn a strong
faith is to endure great trials.
I have learned my faith
by standing firm amid
the most severe of tests.

—

George Mueller

Today's Timely Tip

Talk about it. If you're having tough times, don't hit the panic button and don't keep everything bottled up inside. Find a person you can really trust, and talk things over. A second opinion (or, for that matter, a third, fourth, or fifth opinion) is usually helpful.

Today's Prayer

Heavenly Father, You are my strength and refuge. I can face the difficulties of this day because You are with me. You are my light and pathway. As I follow You, Father, I can overcome adversity just as Jesus overcame this world. Amen

TRUSTING GOD'S TIMING

*Wait for the Lord; be courageous
and let your heart be strong.
Wait for the Lord.*

—

Psalm 27:14 HCSB

Students, as a whole, can be quite an impatient lot. They can't wait for class to end; ditto for the school day and the school week. They wait impatiently for Christmas vacation, spring break, and—most urgently—summer vacation. But, wise teachers understand that life beyond the classroom requires patience, patience, and more patience.

Unlike the precisely charted school year, life unfolds according to a timetable that is ordained, not by man, but by God. Let us, as believers, wait patiently for God, and let us teach patience to those who look to us for guidance . . . even if they're squirming in their seats, waiting for the bell to ring.

Wisdom from God's Holy Word

He said to them, "It is not for you to know times or periods that the Father has set by His own authority."

Acts 1:7 HCSB

He has made everything appropriate in its time. He has also put eternity in their hearts, but man cannot discover the work God has done from beginning to end.

Ecclesiastes 3:11 HCSB

Therefore the Lord is waiting to show you mercy, and is rising up to show you compassion, for the Lord is a just God. Happy are all who wait patiently for Him.

Isaiah 30:18 HCSB

But those who wait on the LORD shall renew their strength; they shall mount up with wings like eagles, they shall run and not be weary, they shall walk and not faint.

Isaiah 40:31 NKJV

More Great Ideas

When we read of the great Biblical leaders, we see that it was not uncommon for God to ask them to wait, not just a day or two, but for years, until God was ready for them to act.

Gloria Gaither

God's delays and His ways can be confusing because the process God uses to accomplish His will can go against human logic and common sense.

Anne Graham Lotz

God is in no hurry. Compared to the works of mankind, He is extremely deliberate. God is not a slave to the human clock.

Charles Swindoll

When God's people believe and pray, the Lord will provide, but we must learn to wait on him with faithful, obedient hearts until the answer comes.

Jim Cymbala

It's safe to trust God's methods
and to go by His clock.

—

S. D. Gordon

Today's Timely Tip

Tough Times 101: Sometimes, when we encounter tough times, we find ourselves "starting over." From scratch. As believers we can find comfort in the knowledge that wherever we find ourselves, whether on the mountaintops of life or in the deepest valleys of despair, God is there with us. And just as importantly, we never have to "start over" with Him, because He never left us!

Today's Prayer

Lord, my sense of timing is fallible and imperfect; Yours is not. Let me trust in Your timetable for my life, and give me the patience and the wisdom to trust Your plans, not my own. Amen

YOUR VERY BRIGHT FUTURE

For I know the thoughts that I think toward you,
says the Lord, thoughts of peace and not of evil,
to give you a future and a hope.
Then you will call upon Me and go and pray
to Me, and I will listen to you.

—

Jeremiah 29:11-12 NKJV

A s you consider God's unfolding plans for your life, you will undoubtedly look to the future . . . after all, the future is where those plans will take place. But sometimes, the future may seem foreboding indeed.

In these uncertain times, it's easy to lose faith in the possibility of a better tomorrow . . . but it's wrong. God instructs us to trust His wisdom, His plan, and His love. When we do so, the future becomes a glorious opportunity to help others, to praise our Creator, and to share God's Good News.

Do you have faith in the ultimate goodness of God's plan? You should. And, do you have faith in the abundant opportunities that await your students? Hopefully, you do. After all, the confidence that you display in your students can be contagious: Your belief in them can have a profound impact on the way they view themselves and their world.

Today, as you stand before your classroom, help your students face the future with optimism, hope, and self-confidence. After all, even in these uncertain times, God still has the last word. And His love endures to all generations, including this one.

Wisdom from God's Holy Word

Do not boast about tomorrow, for you do not know what a day may bring forth.

Proverbs 27:1 NKJV

Remember this: the person who sows sparingly will also reap sparingly, and the person who sows generously will also reap generously.

2 Corinthians 9:6 HCSB

"He has dispersed abroad, He has given to the poor; His righteousness endures forever; His horn will be exalted with honor."

Psalm 112:9 NKJV

Lord, I turn my hope to You. My God, I trust in You.

Psalm 25:1-2 HCSB

More Great Ideas

Yesterday is just experience but tomorrow is glistening with purpose—and today is the channel leading from one to the other.

Barbara Johnson

Do not limit the limitless God! With Him, face the future unafraid because you are never alone.

Mrs. Charles E. Cowman

Take courage. We walk in the wilderness to-day and in the Promised Land tomorrow.

D. L. Moody

We spend our lives dreaming of the future, not realizing that a little of it slips away every day.

Barbara Johnson

We need to be at peace with our past, content with our present, and sure about our future, knowing they are all in God's hands.

Joyce Meyer

Go forward confidently,
energetically attacking
problems, expecting
favorable outcomes.

—

Norman Vincent Peale

Today's Timely Tip

The future isn't some pie-in-the-sky dream. Hope for the future is simply one aspect of trusting God.

Today's Prayer

Dear Lord, as I look to the future, I will place my trust in You. If I become discouraged, I will turn to You. If I am afraid, I will seek strength in You. You are my Father, and I will place my hope, my trust, and my faith in You. Amen

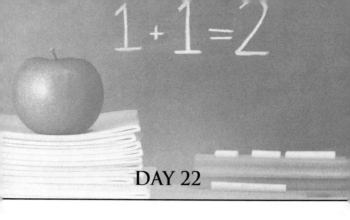

BIG OPPORTUNITIES

*Therefore, as we have opportunity,
we must work for the good of all, especially
for those who belong to the household of faith.*

—

Galatians 6:10 HCSB

As you look at the landscape of your life, do you see opportunities, possibilities, and blessings, or do you focus, instead, upon the more negative scenery? Do you spend more time counting your blessings or your misfortunes? If you've acquired the unfortunate habit of focusing too intently upon the negative aspects of life, then your spiritual vision is in need of correction.

Whether you realize it or not, opportunities are whirling around you like stars crossing the night sky: beautiful to observe, but too numerous to count. Yet you may be too concerned with the challenges of everyday living to notice those opportunities. That's why you should slow down occasionally, catch your breath, and focus your thoughts on two things: the talents God has given you and the opportunities that He has placed before you. God is leading you in the direction of those opportunities. Your task is to watch carefully, to pray fervently, and to act accordingly.

Are you willing to place your future in the hands of a loving and all-knowing God? Do you trust in the ultimate goodness of His plan for your life? Will you face today's challenges with optimism and hope? You should. After all, God created you for a very important purpose: His purpose. And you still have important work to do: His work. And the time to start doing that work is now.

Wisdom from God's Holy Word

Great is Your faithfulness.

Lamentations 3:23 NKJV

Give thanks to Him and praise His name. For the Lord is good, and His love is eternal; His faithfulness endures through all generations.

Psalm 100:4-5 HCSB

A man's heart plans his way, but the Lord determines his steps.

Proverbs 16:9 HCSB

I will instruct you and teach you in the way you should go; I will guide you with My eye.

Psalm 32:8 NKJV

More Great Ideas

Great opportunities often disguise themselves in small tasks.

Rick Warren

A wise man makes more opportunities than he finds.

Francis Bacon

Lovely, complicated wrappings / Sheath the gift of one-day-more; / Breathless, I untie the package— / Never lived this day before!

Gloria Gaither

He who waits until circumstances completely favor his undertaking will never accomplish anything.

Martin Luther

God surrounds you with opportunity. You and I are free in Jesus Christ, not to do whatever we want, but to be all that God wants us to be.

Warren Wiersbe

He who waits until circumstances completely favor his undertaking will never accomplish anything.

—

Martin Luther

Today's Timely Tip

The world of tomorrow is filled with opportunities for those who are willing to find them and work for them. Make certain that you have more than a passing familiarity with the ever shifting sands of our changing world. Then, share your insights with the young people under your care.

Today's Prayer

Lord, as I take the next steps on my life's journey, let me take them with You. Whatever this day may bring, I thank You for the opportunity to live abundantly. Let me lean upon You, Father—and trust You—this day and forever. Amen

COUNTING YOUR BLESSINGS

The Lord bless you and protect you;
the Lord make His face shine on you,
and be gracious to you.

—

Numbers 6:24-25 HCSB

Have you counted your blessings lately? If you sincerely wish to follow in Christ's footsteps, you should make thanksgiving a habit, a regular part of your daily routine.

How has God blessed you? First and foremost, He has given you the gift of eternal life through the sacrifice of His only begotten Son, but the blessings don't stop there. Today, take time to make a partial list of God's gifts to you: the talents, the opportunities, the possessions, and the relationships that you may, on occasion, take for granted. And then, when you've spent sufficient time listing your blessings, offer a prayer gratitude to the Giver of all things good . . . and, to the best of your ability, use your gifts for the glory of His kingdom. When you do, God will smile . . . and so will your students.

Wisdom from God's Holy Word

You will show me the path of life; in Your presence is fullness of joy; at Your right hand are pleasures forevermore.

Psalm 16:11 NKJV

I will make you a great nation; I will bless you and make your name great; and you shall be a blessing. I will bless those who bless you, and I will curse him who curses you; and in you all the families of the earth shall be blessed.

Genesis 12:2-3 NKJV

Blessed is a man who endures trials, because when he passes the test he will receive the crown of life that He has promised to those who love Him.

James 1:12 HCSB

I will make them and the area around My hill a blessing: I will send down showers in their season—showers of blessing.

Ezekiel 34:26 HCSB

More Great Ideas

When God blesses us, He expects us to use those blessings to bless the lives of others.

Jim Gallery

We prevent God from giving us the great spiritual gifts He has in store for us, because we do not give thanks for daily gifts.

Dietrich Bonhoeffer

The Christian life is motivated, not by a list of do's and don'ts, but by the gracious outpouring of God's love and blessing.

Anne Graham Lotz

God blesses us in spite of our lives and not because of our lives.

Max Lucado

Blessings can either humble us and draw us closer to God or allow us to become full of pride and self-sufficiency.

Jim Cymbala

When you live
a surrendered life,
God is willing and able to
provide for your every need.

—

Corrie ten Boom

Today's Timely Tip

Carve out time to thank God for His blessings. Take time out of every day (not just on Sundays) to praise God and thank Him for His gifts.

Today's Prayer

Today, Lord, let me count my blessings with thanksgiving in my heart. You have cared for me, Lord, and I will give You the glory and the praise. Let me accept Your blessings and Your gifts, and let me share them with my students, just as You first shared them with me. Amen

KEEP GROWING!

*But grow in the grace and knowledge
of our Lord and Savior Jesus Christ.
To Him be the glory both now
and to the day of eternity.*

—

2 Peter 3:18 HCSB

The journey toward spiritual maturity lasts a lifetime: As Christians, we can and should continue to grow in the love and the knowledge of our Savior as long as we live. When we cease to grow, either emotionally or spiritually, we do ourselves and our loved ones a profound disservice. But, if we study God's Word, if we obey His commandments, and if we live in the center of His will, we will not be "stagnant" believers; we will, instead, be growing Christians . . . and that's exactly what God wants for our lives.

Many of life's most important lessons are painful to learn. During times of heartbreak and hardship, God stands ready to protect us. As Psalm 147 promises, "He heals the broken-hearted and bandages their wounds" (NCV). In His own time and according to His master plan, God will heal us if we invite Him into our hearts.

Spiritual growth need not take place only in times of adversity. We must seek to grow in our knowledge and love of the Lord every day that we live. In those quiet moments when we open our hearts to God, the One who made us keeps remaking us. He gives us direction, perspective, wisdom, and courage. The appropriate moment to accept those spiritual gifts is the present one.

Wisdom from God's Holy Word

I want their hearts to be encouraged and joined together in love, so that they may have all the riches of assured understanding, and have the knowledge of God's mystery—Christ.

Colossians 2:2 HCSB

Therefore, leaving the elementary message about the Messiah, let us go on to maturity.

Hebrews 6:1 HCSB

For You, O God, have tested us; You have refined us as silver is refined. You brought us into the net; You laid affliction on our backs. You have caused men to ride over our heads; we went through fire and through water; but You brought us out to rich fulfillment.

Psalm 66:10–12 NKJV

More Great Ideas

We are either the masters or the victims of our attitudes. It is a matter of personal choice. Who we are today is the result of choices we made yesterday. Tomorrow, we will become what we choose today. To change means to choose to change.

John Maxwell

Recently I've been learning that life comes down to this: God is in everything. Regardless of what difficulties I am experiencing at the moment, or what things aren't as would like them to be, I look at the circumstances and say, "Lord, what are you trying to teach me?"

Catherine Marshall

There is wonderful freedom and joy in coming to recognize that the fun is in the becoming.

Gloria Gaither

A person who gazes and keeps on gazing at Jesus becomes like him in appearance.

E. Stanley Jones

A Christian is never
in a state of completion
but always in the process
of becoming.

—

Martin Luther

Today's Timely Tip

Times of change can be times of growth. Elisabeth Elliot reminds us that tough times can lead to a renewal of spirit: "If the leaves had not been let go to fall and wither, if the tree had not consented to be a skeleton for many months, there would be no new life rising, no bud, no flower, no fruit, no seed, no new generation."

Today's Prayer

Heavenly Father, I want to grow closer to You each day. I know that obedience to Your will strengthens my relationship with You, so help me to follow Your commandments and obey Your Word today . . . and every day of my life. Amen

AND THE GREATEST
OF THESE . . .

Now these three remain: faith, hope, and love.
But the greatest of these is love.

—

1 Corinthians 13:13 HCSB

God's love changes lives. And as Christian teachers who have received the priceless gift of God's grace, we must make certain that our students can clearly see the changes that God has made in us.

Can we be perfect role models? Of course not. Can we, at all times, be patient, kind, calm, and loving? That's highly unlikely. What we can do is this: we can demonstrate to our students that Christ's love does indeed make a difference in our own lives.

God loved this world so much that He sent His Son to save it. And now only one real question remains for each of us: what will we do in response to God's love? The answer should be obvious: we must allow Christ to reign over our hearts and our lives.

God's grace is the ultimate gift, and we owe Him the ultimate in thanksgiving. Let us praise the Creator for His priceless gift, let us share His Good News, and let us live according to His commandments. When we do, our students will be blessed with powerful, godly role models. As Christian teachers, we must do no less.

Wisdom from God's Holy Word

I pray that you, being rooted and firmly established in love, may be able to comprehend with all the saints what is the breadth and width, height and depth, and to know the Messiah's love that surpasses knowledge, so you may be filled with all the fullness of God.

Ephesians 3:17-19 HCSB

If I speak the languages of men and of angels, but do not have love, I am a sounding gong or a clanging cymbal. If I have the gift of prophecy, and understand all mysteries and all knowledge, and if I have all faith, so that I can move mountains, but do not have love, I am nothing.

1 Corinthians 13:1-2 HCSB

Dear friends, if God loved us in this way, we also must love one another.

1 John 4:11 HCSB

157

More Great Ideas

Hope looks for the good in people, opens doors for people, discovers what can be done to help, lights a candle, does not yield to cynicism. Hope sets people free.

Barbara Johnson

Prayer is the ultimate love language. It communicates in ways we can't.

Stormie Omartian

God loves these people too, just because they're unattractive or warped in their thinking doesn't mean the Lord doesn't love them. And if we don't take them, who is going to take them?

Ruth Bell Graham

We have the Lord, but He Himself has recognized that we need the touch of a human hand. He Himself came down and lived among us as a man. We cannot see Him now, but blessed be the tie that binds human hearts in Christian love.

Vance Havner

Give me such love for
God and men as will blot out
all hatred and bitterness.

—

Dietrich Bonhoeffer

Today's Timely Tip

Be creative. There are many ways to say, "I love you." Find them. Use them. And keep using them.

Today's Prayer

Dear Lord, I will acknowledge Your love; I will accept Your love; and I will share Your love. Let the love that I feel in my heart be expressed through kind words, good deeds and heartfelt prayers. Amen

GOD'S LOVE

But God demonstrates His own love toward us,
in that while we were still sinners,
Christ died for us.

—

Romans 5:8 NKJV

God's love changes lives. And as Christian teachers who have received the priceless gift of God's grace, we must make certain that our students can clearly see the changes that God has made in us.

Can we be perfect role models? Of course not. Can we, at all times, be patient, kind, calm, and loving? That's highly unlikely. What we can do is this: we can demonstrate to our students that Christ's love does indeed make a difference in our own lives.

God loved this world so much that He sent His Son to save it. And now only one real question remains for each of us: what will we do in response to God's love? The answer should be obvious: we must allow Christ to reign over our hearts and our lives.

God's grace is the ultimate gift, and we owe Him the ultimate in thanksgiving. Let us praise the Creator for His priceless gift, let us share His Good News, and let us live according to His commandments. When we do, our students will be blessed with powerful, godly role models. As Christian teachers, we must do no less.

Wisdom from God's Holy Word

May he be blessed by the Lord, who has not forsaken his kindness to the living or the dead.

Ruth 2:20 HCSB

For God loved the world in this way: He gave His only Son, so that everyone who believes in Him will not perish but have eternal life.

John 3:16 HCSB

Whoever is wise will observe these things, and they will understand the lovingkindness of the Lord.

Psalm 107:43 NKJV

But God, who is abundant in mercy, because of His great love that He had for us, made us alive with the Messiah even though we were dead in trespasses. By grace you are saved!

Ephesians 2:4-5 HCSB

We love Him because He first loved us.

1 John 4:19 NKJV

More Great Ideas

There is no pit so deep that God's love is not deeper still.

Corrie ten Boom

I love Him because He first loved me, and He still does love me, and He will love me forever and ever.

Bill Bright

Every tiny bit of my life that has value I owe to the redemption of Jesus Christ. Am I doing anything to enable Him to bring His redemption into evident reality in the lives of others?

Oswald Chambers

It was not the soldiers who killed him, nor the screams of the mob: It was his devotion to us.

Max Lucado

God loves us the way we are, but He loves us too much to leave us that way.

Leighton Ford

God loves each of us
as if there were
only one of us.

—

St. Augustine

Today's Timely Tip

Demonstrate the importance of your relationship with God by spending time with Him each day. And take time each day to share God's love with your family and friends.

Today's Prayer

Thank You, Lord, for Your love. Your love is boundless, infinite, and eternal. Today, let me pause and reflect upon Your love for me, and let me share that love with all those who cross my path. And, as an expression of my love for You, Father, let me share the saving message of Your Son with a world in desperate need of His peace. Amen

GOD'S PLAN
FOR YOU

A man's heart plans his way,
but the Lord directs his steps.

—

Proverbs 16:9 NKJV

Good has a plan for all of us, and as a teacher, you bear a special responsibility for training the students who are entrusted to your care. Because of your position as a guide and mentor, you must be especially careful to seek God's will and to follow it.

God will not force His will upon you. To the contrary, He has given you the free will to follow His commandments . . . or not. If you stray from those commandments, you invite bitter consequences. But, when you choose to follow Him by genuinely and humbly seeking His will, God will touch your heart and lead you on the path of His choosing.

God intends to use you in wonderful, unexpected ways if you let Him, but be forewarned: the decision to seek God's plan and fulfill His purpose is yours and yours alone. The consequences of that decision have profound implications for you and your students, so choose carefully. And then, as you enter the classroom, rest assured that God intends to lead you and use you as a powerful tool for good. Your challenge is to watch for His signs, to obey His commandments, and to follow His path.

Wisdom from God's Holy Word

"For I know the plans I have for you"—[this is] the Lord's declaration—"plans for [your] welfare, not for disaster, to give you a future and a hope."

Jeremiah 29:11 HCSB

We know that all things work together for the good of those who love God: those who are called according to His purpose.

Romans 8:28 HCSB

But as for you, you meant evil against me; but God meant it for good, in order to bring it about as it is this day, to save many people alive.

Genesis 50:20 NKJV

Teach me to do Your will, for You are my God. May Your gracious Spirit lead me on level ground.

Psalm 143:10 HCSB

More Great Ideas

As God's children, we are the recipients of lavish love—a love that motivates us to keep trusting even when we have no idea what God is doing.

Beth Moore

We aren't just thrown on this earth like dice tossed across a table. We are lovingly placed here for a purpose.

Charles Swindoll

Great relief and satisfaction can come from seeking God's priorities for us in each season, discerning what is "best" in the midst of many noble opportunities, and pouring our most excellent energies into those things.

Beth Moore

If not a sparrow falls upon the ground without your Father, you have reason to see that the smallest events of your career and your life are arranged by him.

C. H. Spurgeon

There is no limit
to what God can make us—
if we are willing.

—

Oswald Chambers

Today's Timely Tip

God has a wonderful plan for your life. And the time to start looking for that plan—and living it—is now. And remember—discovering God's plan begins with prayer, but it doesn't end there. You've also got to work at it.

Today's Prayer

Lord, You have a plan for my life that is grander than I can imagine. Let Your purposes be my purposes. Let Your will be my will. When I am confused, give me clarity. When I am frightened, give me courage. Let me be Your faithful servant, always seeking Your guidance for my life. And, let me always be a shining beacon for Your Son today and every day that I live. Amen

EXPERIENCING
GOD'S ABUNDANCE

*I have come that they may have life,
and that they may have it more abundantly.*

—

John 10:10 NKJV

In the 10th chapter of John, when Jesus talks of the abundant life, is He talking about material riches or earthly fame? Hardly. The Son of God came to this world, not to give it prosperity, but to give it salvation. Thankfully for Christians, our Savior's abundance is both spiritual and eternal; it never falters—even if we do—and it never dies. We need only to open our hearts to Him, and His grace becomes ours.

God's gifts are available to all, but those gifts are not guaranteed; God's gifts must be claimed by those who choose to follow Christ. As we go about our daily lives, inside the classroom and out, may we accept God's promise of spiritual abundance, and may we share it with a world in desperate need of the Master's healing touch.

Wisdom from God's Holy Word

And God is able to make every grace overflow to you, so that in every way, always having everything you need, you may excel in every good work.

2 Corinthians 9:8 HCSB

And He said to them, "Take heed and beware of covetousness, for one's life does not consist in the abundance of the things he possesses."

Luke 12:15 NKJV

My cup runs over. Surely goodness and mercy shall follow me all the days of my life; and I will dwell in the house of the Lord forever.

Psalm 23:5-6 NKJV

Until now you have asked for nothing in My name. Ask and you will receive, that your joy may be complete.

John 16:24 HCSB

More Great Ideas

God is the giver, and we are the receivers. And His richest gifts are bestowed not upon those who do the greatest things, but upon those who accept His abundance and His grace.

Hannah Whitall Smith

God's riches are beyond anything we could ask or even dare to imagine! If my life gets gooey and stale, I have no excuse.

Barbara Johnson

It would be wrong to have a "poverty complex," for to think ourselves paupers is to deny either the King's riches or to deny our being His children.

Catherine Marshall

The Bible says that being a Christian is not only a great way to die, but it's also the best way to live.

Bill Hybels

The only way you can
experience abundant life
is to surrender your plans
to Him.

—

Charles Stanley

Today's Timely Tip

God wants to shower you with abundance—
your job is to let Him.

Today's Prayer

Thank You, Father, for the abundant life
that is mine through Christ Jesus. Guide me
according to Your will, and help me to be a
worthy servant in all that I say and do. Give
me courage, Lord, to claim the gifts You have
promised—and give me the wisdom to share
those gifts, today and every day. Amen

BEYOND ANGER

*Everyone must be quick to hear, slow to speak,
and slow to anger, for man's anger does not
accomplish God's righteousness.*

—

James 1:19-20 HCSB

Teaching, like every job, has its fair share of frustrations—some great, and some small. Sometimes, those frustrations may cause you to reach the boiling point. But here's a word of warning: When you're tempted to lose your temper over the minor inconveniences of the teaching profession, don't give voice to your angry thoughts.

When you make haste to speak angry words, you will inevitably say things that you'll soon regret. Remember: God will help you control your temper if you ask Him to do so. And the time to ask Him is before your temper gets the best of you—not after.

Wisdom from God's Holy Word

*A patient person [shows] great understanding, but
a quick-tempered one promotes foolishness.*

Proverbs 14:29 HCSB

*But now you must also put away all the following:
anger, wrath, malice, slander, and filthy language
from your mouth.*

Colossians 3:8 HCSB

*All bitterness, anger and wrath, insult and
slander must be removed from you, along with all
wickedness. And be kind and compassionate to
one another, forgiving one another, just as God
also forgave you in Christ.*

Ephesians 4:31-32 HCSB

*I tell you that on the day of judgment people will
have to account for every careless word they
speak. For by your words you will be acquitted,
and by your words you will be condemned.*

Matthew 12:36-37 HCSB

More Great Ideas

Anger is the noise of the soul; the unseen irritant of the heart; the relentless invader of silence.

Max Lucado

When you strike out in anger, you may miss the other person, but you will always hit yourself.

Jim Gallery

Get rid of the poison of built-up anger and the acid of long-term resentment.

Charles Swindoll

Anger's the anaesthetic of the mind.

C. S. Lewis

Anger breeds remorse in the heart, discord in the home, bitterness in the community, and confusion in the state.

Billy Graham

When something robs you of
your peace of mind,
ask yourself if it is worth
the energy you are expending
on it. If not, then put it out
of your mind in an act of
discipline. Every time
the thought of "it" returns,
refuse it.

—

Kay Arthur

Today's Timely Tip

God's Word warns against the folly and the futility of anger. It's a warning you should take seriously.

Today's Prayer

Lord, sometimes, in moments of frustration, I become angry. When I fall prey to pettiness, restore my sense of perspective. When I fall prey to irrational anger, give me inner calm. Let me show my thankfulness to You by offering forgiveness to others. And, when I do, may others see Your love reflected through my words and my deeds. Amen

DAY 30

A LIFE OF SERVICE

*But he who is greatest among you
shall be your servant.*

—

Matthew 23:11 NKJV

As a teacher, you have chosen a life of service. Congratulations. Jesus teaches that the most esteemed men and women are not the political leaders or the captains of industry. To the contrary, Jesus teaches that the greatest among us are those who choose to minister and to serve.

When you decided to become a teacher, you demonstrated your willingness to serve in a very tangible way. As a result, you can be comforted by the knowledge that your kindness and generosity will touch the lives of students in ways that you may never fully comprehend. But God knows the impact of your good works, and He will bless you because of them.

The words of Galatians 6:9 are clear: "Let us not become weary in doing good, for at the proper time we will reap a harvest if we do not give up" (NIV). May you never grow weary of your role as a teacher, and may your good works continue to bless your students long after the final school bell has rung.

Wisdom from God's Holy Word

The righteous give and don't hold back.

Proverbs 21:26 HCSB

When it is in your power, don't withhold good from the one to whom it is due.

Proverbs 3:27 HCSB

The generous soul will be made rich, and he who waters will also be watered himself.

Proverbs 11:25 NKJV

If anyone serves Me, let him follow Me; and where I am, there My servant will be also. If anyone serves Me, him My Father will honor.

John 12:26 NKJV

Therefore, my dear brothers, be steadfast, immovable, always abounding in the Lord's work, knowing that your labor in the Lord is not in vain.

1 Corinthians 15:58 HCSB

More Great Ideas

I can usually sense that a leading is from the Holy Spirit when it calls me to humble myself, serve somebody, encourage somebody or give something away. Very rarely will the evil one lead us to do those kind of things.

Bill Hybels

So many times we say that we can't serve God because we aren't whatever is needed. We're not talented enough or smart enough or whatever. But if you are in covenant with Jesus Christ, He is responsible for covering your weaknesses, for being your strength. He will give you His abilities for your disabilities!

Kay Arthur

In the great orchestra we call life, you have an instrument and a song, and you owe it to God to play them both sublimely.

Max Lucado

We worship God
through service.
The authentic server views
each opportunity to lead or
serve as an opportunity
to worship God.

—

Bill Hybels

Today's Timely Tip

Christ was a humble servant, and you need to value the importance of following His example. Also, you need to understand that greatness in God's kingdom relates to service, not status.

Today's Prayer

Lord, I can serve only one master; let me serve You. Let my actions be pleasing to You; let my words reflect Your infinite love; let my prayers be sincere and my thoughts be pure. In everything that I do, Father, let me praise You and serve You today and for eternity. Amen

MORE FROM
GOD'S WORD
ABOUT . . .

Anger

A patient person [shows] great understanding, but a quick-tempered one promotes foolishness.

Proverbs 14:29 HCSB

But now you must also put away all the following: anger, wrath, malice, slander, and filthy language from your mouth.

Colossians 3:8 HCSB

All bitterness, anger and wrath, insult and slander must be removed from you, along with all wickedness. And be kind and compassionate to one another, forgiving one another, just as God also forgave you in Christ.

Ephesians 4:31-32 HCSB

Everyone must be quick to hear, slow to speak, and slow to anger, for man's anger does not accomplish God's righteousness.

James 1:19-20 HCSB

*Don't let your spirit rush
to be angry, for anger abides
in the heart of fools.*

—

Ecclesiastes 7:9 HCSB

Attitude

For the word of God is living and effective and sharper than any two-edged sword, penetrating as far as to divide soul, spirit, joints, and marrow; it is a judge of the ideas and thoughts of the heart.

Hebrews 4:12 HCSB

Make your own attitude that of Christ Jesus.

Philippians 2:5 HCSB

Set your minds on what is above, not on what is on the earth.

Colossians 3:2 HCSB

Finally brothers, whatever is true, whatever is honorable, whatever is just, whatever is pure, whatever is lovely, whatever is commendable—if there is any moral excellence and if there is any praise—dwell on these things.

Philippians 4:8 HCSB

Cheerfulness

A merry heart does good, like medicine.

Proverbs 17:22 NKJV

Is anyone cheerful? He should sing praises.

James 5:13 HCSB

A cheerful heart has a continual feast.

Proverbs 15:15 HCSB

Bright eyes cheer the heart; good news strengthens the bones.

Proverbs 15:30 HCSB

A joyful heart makes a face cheerful.

Proverbs 15:13 HCSB

Faith

If you do not stand firm in your faith, then you will not stand at all.

Isaiah 7:9 HCSB

Be alert, stand firm in the faith, be brave and strong.

1 Corinthians 16:13 HCSB

Now faith is the reality of what is hoped for, the proof of what is not seen.

Hebrews 11:1 HCSB

For we walk by faith, not by sight.

2 Corinthians 5:7 HCSB

Now without faith it is impossible to please God, for the one who draws near to Him must believe that He exists and rewards those who seek Him.

Hebrews 11:6 HCSB

Family

Choose for yourselves today the one you will worship . . . . As for me and my family, we will worship the Lord.

Joshua 24:15 HCSB

Now if anyone does not provide for his own relatives, and especially for his household, he has denied the faith and is worse than an unbeliever.

1 Timothy 5:8 HCSB

If a kingdom is divided against itself, that kingdom cannot stand. If a house is divided against itself, that house cannot stand.

Mark 3:24-25 HCSB

Love must be without hypocrisy. Detest evil; cling to what is good. Show family affection to one another with brotherly love. Outdo one another in showing honor.

Romans 12:9–10 HCSB

Loving God

He said to him, "You shall love the Lord your God with all your heart, with all your soul, and with all your mind. This is the greatest and most important commandment."

Matthew 22:37-38 HCSB

And we have this command from Him: the one who loves God must also love his brother.

1 John 4:21 HCSB

Love the Lord your God with all your heart, with all your soul, and with all your strength. These words that I am giving you today are to be in your heart. Repeat them to your children. Talk about them when you sit in your house and when you walk along the road, when you lie down and when you get up.

Deuteronomy 6:5-7 HCSB

For this is the love of God, that we keep His commandments. And His commandments are not burdensome.

1 John 5:3 NKJV

*We love Him
because He first loved us.*

—

1 John 4:19 NKJV

Materialism

And He told them, "Watch out and be on guard against all greed, because one's life is not in the abundance of his possessions."

Luke 12:15 HCSB

For what does it benefit a man to gain the whole world yet lose his life? What can a man give in exchange for his life?

Mark 8:36-37 HCSB

Don't collect for yourselves treasures on earth, where moth and rust destroy and where thieves break in and steal. But collect for yourselves treasures in heaven, where neither moth nor rust destroys, and where thieves don't break in and steal. For where your treasure is, there your heart will be also.

Matthew 6:19-21 HCSB

For the mind-set of the flesh is death, but the mind-set of the Spirit is life and peace.

Romans 8:6 HCSB

*Anyone trusting
in his riches will fall,
but the righteous
will flourish like foliage.*

—

Proverbs 11:28 HCSB

Temptation

No temptation has overtaken you except what is common to humanity. God is faithful and He will not allow you to be tempted beyond what you are able, but with the temptation He will also provide a way of escape, so that you are able to bear it.

1 Corinthians 10:13 HCSB

For we do not have a High Priest who cannot sympathize with our weaknesses, but was in all points tempted as we are, yet without sin. Let us therefore come boldly to the throne of grace, that we may obtain mercy and find grace to help in time of need.

Hebrews 4:15-16 NKJV

Be sober! Be on the alert! Your adversary the Devil is prowling around like a roaring lion, looking for anyone he can devour.

1 Peter 5:8 HCSB

The Lord knows how to deliver the godly out of temptations.

2 Peter 2:9 NKJV

*Put on the whole armor of God,
that you may be able to stand
against the wiles of the devil.*

—

Ephesians 6:11 NKJV

Testimony

But sanctify the Lord God in your hearts, and always be ready to give a defense to everyone who asks you a reason for the hope that is in you.

1 Peter 3:15 HCSB

You are the light of the world. A city that is set on a hill cannot be hidden. Nor do they light a lamp and put it under a basket, but on a lampstand, and it gives light to all who are in the house. Let your light so shine before men, that they may see your good works and glorify your Father in heaven.

Matthew 5:14–16 NKJV

Whatever I tell you in the dark, speak in the light; and what you hear in the ear, preach on the housetops.

Matthew 10:27 NKJV

But as for me, I will never boast about anything except the cross of our Lord Jesus Christ, through whom the world has been crucified to me, and I to the world.

Galatians 6:14 HCSB

And I say to you,
anyone who acknowledges Me
before men, the Son of Man
will also acknowledge him before
the angels of God; but whoever
denies Me before men will be
denied before the angels of God.

—

Luke 12:8-9 HCSB

Thanksgiving

Thanks be to God for His indescribable gift.

2 Corinthians 9:15 HCSB

And let the peace of the Messiah, to which you were also called in one body, control your hearts. Be thankful.

Colossians 3:15 HCSB

It is good to give thanks to the Lord, and to sing praises to Your name, O Most High.

Psalm 92:1 NKJV

Therefore as you have received Christ Jesus the Lord, walk in Him, rooted and built up in Him and established in the faith, just as you were taught, and overflowing with thankfulness.

Colossians 2:6-7 HCSB

Enter into His gates with thanksgiving, and into His courts with praise. Be thankful to Him, and bless His name. For the Lord is good; His mercy is everlasting, and His truth endures to all generations.

Psalm 100:4-5 NKJV

Wisdom

The fear of the Lord is the beginning of wisdom; a good understanding have all those who do His commandments. His praise endures forever.

Psalm 111:10 NKJV

So teach us to number our days, that we may gain a heart of wisdom.

Psalm 90:12 NKJV

A wise man will hear and increase learning, and a man of understanding will attain wise counsel.

Proverbs 1:5 NKJV

Teach me, O Lord, the way of Your statutes, and I shall keep it to the end.

Psalm 119:33 NKJV

Acquire wisdom—how much better it is than gold! And acquire understanding—it is preferable to silver.

Proverbs 16:16 HCSB